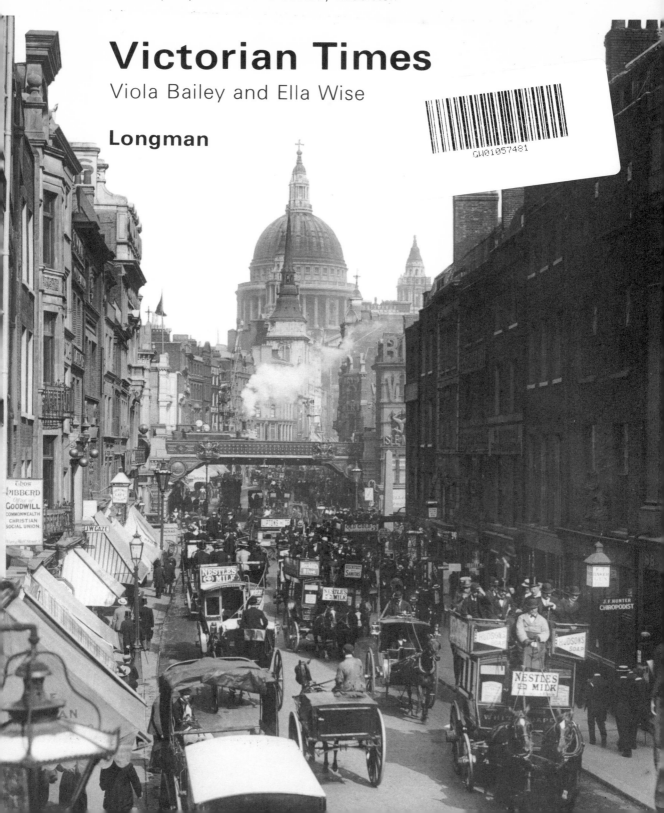

Focus on History

edited by Ray Mitchell and Geoffrey Middleton

Victorian Times

Viola Bailey and Ella Wise

Longman

ELIZABETH II

GEORGE VI

GEORGE V

EDWARD VII

VICTORIA

If this
child
were
you

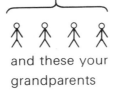

and these
were your
parents

and these your
grandparents

then these 8 were your
great-grandparents

and these 16 were your great-great-grandparents.

Is anything known in your family about these ancestors of yours? Where were they born? Where did they live? What did they do with their lives? Were they rich or were they poor? Where are their graves?

Some of them lived at the time of Queen Victoria. She was the great-great-grandmother of Queen Elizabeth II. Her reign from 1837 to 1901 was the longest in British History. She was born in 1819 so you see she lived through most of the 19th century. This book is about the times in which she lived.

Many Victorians, the Queen and David Livingstone among them, kept Journals in which they wrote down events and matters of interest. As you read through this book you will have much to record, so start a Victorian Journal of your own.

Put the heading
GLOSSARY
on the last two pages
and enter here all
new words you meet,
with their
meanings.

Living in splendour

Here for you to study are modern photographs of three of the many splendid mansions built for the wealthy Victorians. Architects liked to design buildings for them in the styles of the past.

Penrhyn Castle in Wales will remind you of a Norman Castle.

Thoresby Hall in Nottinghamshire has the look of a Tudor mansion. ▶

Alton Towers in Staffordshire could be an abbey or a cathedral.

Some of you may be able to visit these or other great Victorian houses like Eastnor Castle, Hereford; Queen Victoria's Isle of Wight home, Osborne House; Oldway House, Devon; Lancaster House, London; Cliveden, Bucks; Waddesdon Manor, Bucks; and Hughenden Manor, Bucks, the home of Benjamin Disraeli, a famous Victorian Prime Minister.

In your Journal record with notes, sketches and photographs any visits you may make. Add special notes of any Victorian furniture, china, or kitchen equipment which may be on view.

In this picture of Derby Day 1856 we have a glimpse of the wealthy out in their own carriages. The original painting by W. P. Frith may be seen in the Tate Gallery, London. You can learn from this picture something of Victorian fashions and habits at that time. Look for:

— gentlemen in narrow trousers, fancy waistcoats, stand-up collars, raglan-sleeved travelling coats and silk top hats. Some have coloured muslin scarves tied round their hats.

— the footman unpacking a picnic basket. He is setting out on a cloth, lobster, game pie and bread rolls. See the little acrobat hungrily watching him.

— a small boy crawling under the carriage to steal some food

— the elegant young lady in a fine dress with a wide full skirt. This would be held out by a steel cage, called a crinoline, worn underneath. She wears a straw hat with a flat crown. What headgear is worn by the other ladies? Notice their fringed parasols to shield them from the sun. No Victorian lady ever allowed her skin to become tanned.

You can find also:
— gypsies with their children. A woman with a baby begging for money
— a countryman wearing a smock and a hat with a low crown and
  broad brim
— the jockeys on their mounts
— the young man who has lost all his money betting at the races.
— a barefoot girl selling bunches of flowers.
After the races carrier pigeons would fly the results to the big towns.

The Victorians liked pictures which appealed to their feelings.
From the picture of Derby Day, find examples of people who look
bored, excited or desperate. Which people do you feel curious about,
amused at, or sorry for?

Now write the heading 'FASHIONS' on several pages in your
Journal. On the first of these pages sketch, from Derby Day, items of
fashion like crinolines, hats, a countryman's smock, parasols. As you read
on through this book continue to make sketches of fashions you see in
the pictures. Label and date every sketch.

The elegant young ladies in the picture on pages 4 and 5 lived in surroundings like these. This is the Blue Drawing Room at Thoresby Hall. Look at:

— the walls covered with patterned silk which was blue and which gave the room its name
— the 2 cut-glass candle chandeliers
— the large gilt mirror over the only fireplace in this large room
— the satin-covered ottoman of 4 seats in the centre of the room
— the rich ceiling decorated in a style known as 'Rococo'
— the 19th century portraits of the owners the Earl and Countess Manvers
— the grand piano in the corner on the right. It has a lace cover, on which stand photographs and vases.

Before the days of radio and television, the piano was important to every drawing room. Here family and friends were entertained in the evenings. Young ladies were taught to play the piano, and both young ladies and young gentlemen were taught to sing.

On page 6 you saw that candle chandeliers were used to light the Blue Drawing Room at Thoresby Hall. This is how the Velvet Drawing Room in another great house, Saltram, Devon, was lit in the 19th century. The chandelier, made about 1830, at first burnt colza oil. This was made from the crushed seeds of the rape plant. After 1859 when oilfields in Pennsylvania, U.S.A., were opened, paraffin oil could be used in lamps.

By 1880 some people were trying out the new electric lighting. Lord Salisbury in 1881 used a water wheel to generate electric current. His home at Hatfield was the first of the great country houses to be lit by electricity.

The wealthy loved to entertain in their splendid homes. Here you are looking at the dining room at Tatton Park, Cheshire. The table is arranged for a dinner party.

At the fashionable dinner parties, footmen dressed in livery (uniform) and wearing white gloves and stockings waited at table. Their livery has long ago worn out but buttons from it can still be found in old button boxes and junk shops. The two shown here are silver. They bear the crests of the families for whom the footmen worked.

The dinner services were often of 400 pieces. They were made of fine china such as Minton, Coalport, Crown Derby, Copeland, Rockingham or Royal Worcester. All the best china had a special mark on the underside of each piece. On the back of this Royal Worcester plate is this mark.

Find on it
    a crown,
        a circle,
            4 Ws and
                a crescent. This is the factory mark.
The number 51 is for 1751 when the factory began. The letter D stands for 1870, the year the plate was made. Copy this mark and its meaning into your Journal.

Someone among your relations or family friends may have a piece of Victorian china. Ask if you may sketch it and copy the mark on it. If you are interested you can find a key to the marks of the main factories in the book: *Victorian Porcelain* by G. A. Godden, which is in most public libraries.

...use for a moment ...er this Victorian ...droom. Here early ...e June morning ...1837, Princess ...ctoria, aged 18, ...as awakened to hear ...at she was Queen. ...er uncle, King ...illiam IV, was dead ...d she was next in ...e to the throne.

Did you notice the ...all china basin and ...g in the far corner? ...here was no piped hot ...d cold water then ...Kensington Palace. ...he usual way of ...king a bath was in a shallow hip bath placed in the bedroom. The water ...r this was brought up in cans from the kitchens by the servants.

Here is a picture of one of the earliest bathrooms. It was a ...nsation in 1825. Can you find the bath? Before Victoria became ...ueen it was rare to have a bathroom even in a palace. Windsor ...astle had none until 1847. The bath in the picture was made of copper. ...ater was pumped up from the kitchen and there was a waste pipe to

carry it away. This bathroom was in the fine town house of an architect, Sir John Soane, at 13, Lincoln's Inn Fields, London. The house and its treasures are now the Sir John Soane's Museum. Town houses like Sir John's could draw water from the piped street supply, and pump it into storage tanks.

In this kitchen
the lady of
the house is
talking to her
chief servant,
the butler.
Look at:
— the lady's
dress. She
wears the
latest fashion
of the 1880s
the bustle.
This was a
cage of steel or horse-hair worn behind and under the dress.
— the cook and the maids wearing dresses of cotton print, caps and
aprons. Cotton cloth from the mills in Lancashire was cheap at this time.
— a housemaid with a broom. There were no electric cleaners and
floors and carpets had to be brushed clean. Once a year carpets were
lifted outside and beaten
— the large clothes-horse in the background where sheets are airing
in front of a kitchen range.

The fine Victorian range pictured here
shows ovens and hot plates for cooking
and a tap for drawing hot water from
the boiler.

The great houses needed from 30 to
50 (or more) indoor servants. These
were divided into 'upper' servants like
butlers, cooks, housekeepers, footmen,
coachmen (who had their own dining
and sitting rooms), and 'lower' servants.
Outside there would be grooms and yard
lads who slept over the stables. The
gardeners had living quarters known as the 'bothy'. Many
of these servants came from the families of the farm labourers
and were usually employed by the age of 10.

The country poor

This picture shows you a scene on board a sailing ship carrying convicts to Australia. Among thousands of prisoners transported in this way were 6 farm labourers from the village of Tolpuddle in Dorset. You will see the prisoners are crowded into cages. Watching them are armed guards.

The voyage took about 6 months. Do you think the picture shows a calm day at sea? What would it be like in a storm?

There were no medical supplies and the main food was hard, dry, thick ship's biscuits. These were often full of weevils. Some of these men would die on the voyage and be buried at sea.

What crime had the 6 Dorset labourers committed? Their wages had been reduced from 9/– (45p) to 7/– (35p) weekly and one of the men, George Lovelace, had sent to the Grand National Trades Union, led by Robert Owen, for help.

You will know about Trade Unions. At the time of this story the idea of Trade Unions was new. Employers, fearing riots, were nervous of them. So the labourers were arrested, tried under the Mutiny Act, and ordered to be sent to a convict settlement in Australia. People became very angry about this harsh treatment. 800,000 people signed petitions for the release of the Tolpuddle Martyrs as they were called. Finally they were pardoned. George Lovelace was the first to be sent home. The date was June 1837, the very month that Victoria had become Queen.

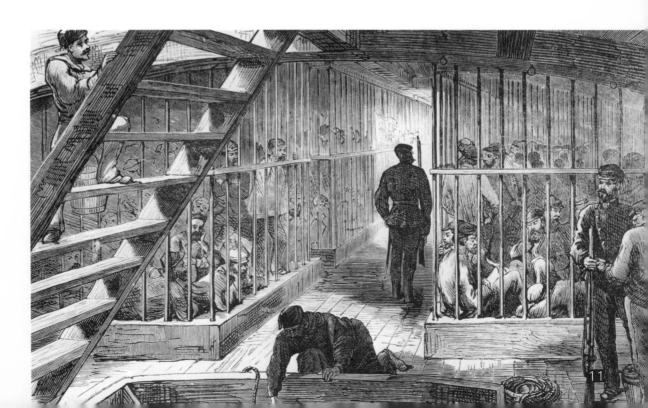

Here you see another farm labourer in trouble. Because his wages
were so low, he had been poaching. Up to the 1850s a man could be
sent to the convict settlements in Australia for this. Thomas Rowlandson
painted this story picture to show:

— a landowner, a Justice of the Peace, seated at the table
— five angry men bringing in Joseph Tomms, a poacher, handcuffed
— a gamekeeper with the hare Joseph had snared
— Joseph's wife and child on their knees begging for mercy. What
  would happen to them if Joseph were to be transported? Perhaps the
  poacher's wife could earn a little by working in the fields.

What field work is this woman doing? She is making a hole
with a 'dibber'. In her right hand she holds some large seeds,
perhaps broad beans, which she is planting. Imagine being
bent over this work all day for one penny an hour. There was
no waterproof clothing and she would often be soaked by rain.
Her heavy leather boots would be stiff and hard from many
dryings.

From an encyclopaedia find out more about poaching. Then
make Joseph's story into a play to act with your friends.

Now read these entries taken from Victorian school log books. (A school log book is a kind of diary kept by the head teacher.)

'June 26 1866   25 children in fields singling (thinning) beet.'

'April 21 1868   Alice Walford detained at home for sometime her mother going into the fields to work.'

'April 23 1877   Many of the boys absent working in the fields.'

'April 24 1885   Children kept away to pick stones.'

(These were used for filling holes in the roads.)

Why were these children absent from school on the dates given? These were all young children, for most labourers' children had left school by the age of 10.

Here is the weekly budget of a labourer, Robert Crick, his wife and 5 children in the 1840s. Copy it into your Journal with a suitable title:

NAME	AGE	EARNINGS	EXPENDITURE	
Robert Crick	42	9s 0d	Bread (27 large)	9s 0d
			Potatoes	1s 0d
His wife	40	9d	Rent	1s 2d
			Tea	2d
His son	12	2s 0d	Sugar ($\frac{1}{2}$lb)	$3\frac{1}{2}$d
			Soap	3d
His son	11	1s 0d	Blue	$\frac{1}{2}$d
			Thread etc.	2d
His son	8	1s 0d	Candles (6)	3d
			Salt	$\frac{1}{2}$d
His daughter	6		Coal and wood	9d
			Butter ($\frac{1}{2}$lb)	$4\frac{1}{2}$d
His son	4		Cheese ($\frac{1}{2}$lb)	3d
		13s 9d (69p)		13s 9d

This was the budget of a careful man who had had some schooling.
Find out:

— on which item most money was spent

— what was used for lighting in this home

— if there was any allowance for meat, clothes, boots, savings, toys, books, medicine or amusements.

Penny sticks of opium could be bought to ease the pain from rheumatism caused by the cold, damp, poor food and clothing, and exhaustion. Mothers who went out to work often gave their babies sips of a brew called Godfrey's Cordial, which contained opium and treacle. This made the babies sleep.

Study this paragraph from a report made by Sir James Caird in 1850, then list in your Journal the food this Dorset labourer had for each of his 4 daily meals. Arrange the list in columns.

'After doing up his horses, he takes breakfast, which is made of flour with a little butter and water from the tea-kettle poured over it. He takes with him to the field a piece of bread and (if he has not a growing family, and can afford it) cheese to eat midday. He returns home in the afternoon to a few potatoes, and possibly a little bacon, though only those who are better off can afford this. The supper very commonly consists of bread and water.'

If one of your ancestors had been a farm labourer he might have brought up a large family, crowded into a two-roomed cottage like one of those above. The next picture shows the excellent cottages built for workers on his estates in Suffolk and Cheshire by a good landowner, Lord John Tollemache. Each of his cottages had land for growing vegetables, keeping chickens or rearing animals.

What happened to the farm labourer and his wife when they became too old or too ill to work? They had to go to a Workhouse. This was a house of shelter for the poor. You may wonder why it was called a Workhouse. The name arose because all who could work were given work to do there.

Some parishes united to build a workhouse which they called a 'Union'. These 19th century buildings are often used now as hospitals or homes for old people. Find out if there is an old workhouse building in your district. If so, for what is it used?

You see here a farm labourer sharpening a tool called a scythe. Before the invention of farm machinery men used scythes to mow the fields at harvest time. Think what heavy labour it was, and what skill was needed, to swing a scythe like this from dawn to dusk.

Now look at the reaping machine in the second picture. When was it used? These American inventions of the 1850s were soon to be seen in the English harvest fields.

What do we call the village craftsman in the third picture? He stands proudly beside his latest handiwork. Notice the wheel is fitted with an

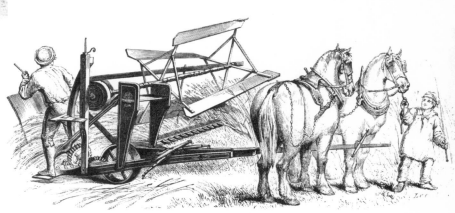

iron rim. Can you think why his skill, like that of the blacksmith and saddler, was in such demand? These men, like stonemasons, carpenters and thatchers made a better living than the farm labourer.

Now imagine you have a letter from an Australian school friend who has discovered that among his Victorian ancestors were a sheep farmer, a gold miner and a poacher who had been transported from England. He wants to know about a farm labourer's life in mid-Victorian England. Answer his letter, using this plan:
Living conditions, Wages, Work, Poaching Laws, Old Age. Add sketches to make your letter more interesting.

ENGLISH HARVEST-HOME.

Where is this supper being held? What kind of people are there?
What food and drink are being served? It was the custom, when the
harvest had been gathered in, for the farmer to give all his workers
a fine harvest supper or 'Horkey'. You will see in the picture there
are children present. They often stayed away from school to see the
last waggons of corn carted from the fields and to attend the Horkeys.

Westleton School Log Book for 1875 has this entry:

'Sept. 16   There are at least forty children absent today, the
           Harvest Home held at Dunwich being the great attraction.'

From your hymn book find out which Harvest hymns were written in
the 19th century and enter the titles, names of writers and dates in
your Journal.

Young labourers often left their villages and tramped off to the
towns to find better paid jobs. Some found work in the new factories
of the Midlands and the North. As they were used to the fresh air of the
fields they found factory work a threat to health. For instance, in
Sheffield men worked on the grinding of knife blades. They breathed
in the dry metal dust. This killed many of them before they were 35.

Town life

Working class dwellings

As people crowded into the towns for work, it became hard to find somewhere to live. Read the notices on the houses in this picture. You can see that too many people living here in old houses with no water supply, no sanitation and no refuse collection — have made the place a slum.

A shortage of houses for workers was a big problem in fast-growing towns like Liverpool, Manchester, Bolton, Oldham, Preston, Bradford, Leeds, Halifax, Birmingham, Sheffield and Glasgow.

If you live in a town look for a row of Victorian houses like these. They were built in Manchester in 1870 for working class families. Notice:

— the doors open on to the pavement
— the number of chimneys on these small houses. (Here you have the clue to the fuel used for cooking and heating.)
— the stone paving used for the road.

To help solve the housing problem in some towns, great blocks of working men's flats were built. In London the Peabody Buildings were built with money given by a rich American, George Peabody.

Middle class homes   This picture shows you one of a row of better class houses. Here lived people like doctors, solicitors and business men with their large families, servants and many possessions. They were part of the middle class in Victorian life. The room in the next picture could be a sitting room in one of these houses. Everything is decorated or carved and every surface crowded with objects.

Find: a heavily carved straight-backed chair, the patterned carpet, an overmantel with mirror, a fire screen, a gas lamp on a bracket, a clock, an oil lamp, photographs on the wall, a table-cloth, lace curtains, a window blind, dried flowers in a vase, a stuffed animal in a glass case, an aspidistra plant on a stand, a photograph album, bellows, an harmonium, and 17 vases.

Write your own description of this room with the title, VICTORIAN SITTING ROOM, and sketch some of its contents.

Find a picture of a modern room for the next page and describe the differences between the two rooms in lighting, heating, furnishing and items for entertainment

een in the streets In the streets of the Victorian towns many people struggled to make a living. Here is a street photographer. The camera was a 19th century invention. It recorded for us, for the first time in history, people, places and events as they really were. The name of William ox-Talbot is famous in the history of photography. From n encyclopaedia find out all you can about him. Write your ndings in your Journal.

Now look at the photograph below. What is the man in the owler hat selling from his barrow? Immigrants from cily ran the street ice-cream business. They hired out the arrows and the freezing machines for making the okey-Pokey' as it was called. The ice-cream was often ade in the overcrowded single room where the Hokey-Pokey ohnny and all his family lived and slept. Look at the

thick glasses which hold the ices sold at half-a-penny each. These glasses were washed in a bucket kept under the cart. They were then dried on a cloth. Can you imagine what the water in the bucket and the cloth were like at the end of a busy day? Take a close look at the clothes, footwear and headgear of the children. These were photographed in the streets of Greenwich on a summer's day in the 1880s.

This barefoot lad, also photographed in Greenwich, is selling matches at half-a-penny a box. What are they called? Who are the makers? Do they still make matches? Yellow phosphorous used in their manufacture caused a dreaded disease known as 'Phossy Jaw'. Gather information on the making of matches and write notes on this in your Journal.

How is milk delivered to your home? Last century it could have been brought by this bowler-hatted, blue-aproned milkman pushing a cart. For whom does this milkman work? His churn of a zinc-type metal holds 17 gallons (77 litres). He has a can for measuring out milk into the customer's jug.

In the poorer districts of the town the streets were the children's playground. How are these children amusing themselves? Do you, by law, have to attend school? Before 1880 there was no law to make all children in England and Wales attend school.

The unwanted On this page and the next are actual photographs of some of the thousands of destitute and homeless children who lived in the streets of the great Victorian towns. These dirty, ragged children slept under stacks of old boxes and upturned boats. They huddled in doorways, in barrels, and one is known to have slept in the grass roller in a London Park.

Why were so many children homeless? There were many reasons. Some were the children of convicts in prison. Some had fled from workhouses where they had been bullied and beaten, or from drunken mothers and fathers. There were in the streets, children who had run away from cruel working conditions in which they had been placed by their parents. Why? Sickness, accidents, low wages, unemployment, were some of the reasons why parents could not keep their children. Don't forget that in Victorian times there was no National Health Service, no National Assistance, no Children's Allowances, no Unemployment Benefit and no State Pensions.

As you read this there are still boys and girls in parts of Europe, Asia and South America who never go to school. Some, like the Victorian unwanted children, have run away, or have been put out to work at an early age. The little they earn is needed by their poverty-stricken families. A famous Victorian writer Charles Dickens tells sad stories of unwanted children in his books *Oliver Twist* and *Nicholas Nickleby*.

This homeless boy was lucky to find someone who cared, Thomas Barnardo. As a young man of 19, he had come from Ireland in 1865 to study medicine at the London Hospital in the Whitechapel Road. In the evenings he worked in an old donkey stable in Hope Place, Stepney, where ragged urchins came to learn to read.

One evening a youngster named Jim Jarvis asked to be allowed to sleep in the stable. He told Barnardo that he and hundreds like him had no homes and nowhere to go. Barnardo had wanted to be a missionary in China but he saw there was much work to be done in London and other big towns. In his lifetime he opened 35 homes for children in Britain, 2 in Canada, and 43 other centres of help. Today there are 103 homes and special schools in Britain, 12 in Australia and 1 in Kenya.

The pictures on pages 21 and 22 come from the records of Dr. Barnardo's Homes. Have you thought that even today children are made homeless by accident or disaster? Ask for and read the book: *Dr. Barnardo*, by N. Wymer.

Very few of the needy children could read or write. Some people who cared started schools (known as Ragged Schools) for them. Their greatest supporter was the Earl of Shaftesbury. In Parliament he worked for all ill-treated children. There were the young climbing boys, who were sometimes burnt or suffocated climbing up and sweeping inside the narrow Victorian chimneys. There were children working long hours in factories and mines in Wales, the Midlands and the North of England. Another book called *The Factory Age* in the *Focus On History* Series will tell you about the working lives of these children.

What is the name of the school shown in this picture?
Notice that most of the children are barefooted. The need
to care for these children and to provide work for the
older ones led to Shaftesbury starting:
— refuges for homeless children like
  the girl and her baby brother
  in the photograph. They were
  found abandoned in the streets.
— orphanages for the very young
— the Arethusa Training Ship
  (a Naval Training School)
— a Newsboys' Lodging House
— homes for cripples
— a Shoeblacks' Brigade.

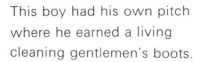

This boy had his own pitch
where he earned a living
cleaning gentlemen's boots.

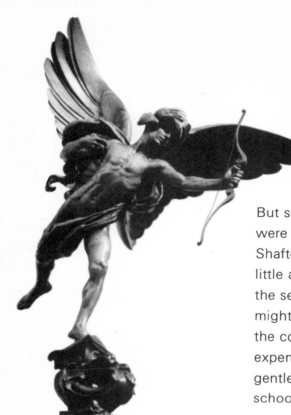

You may have seen in the centre of Piccadilly Circus, London, this aluminium statue of a winged archer. It was set up there in memory of the Earl of Shaftesbury and his work for the suffering and needy in the 19th century. People christened the statue 'Eros'. There is still a Shaftesbury Society carrying on his fine work.

But should you think the only suffering children were those who were poor, read these facts about Shaftesbury's childhood. His parents cared little about him and left him to the mercy of the servants. But for one, Maria Millis, he might have starved to death or perished from the cold. At the age of 7 he was sent away to an expensive boarding school run for the sons of gentlemen. In later life he wrote about that school:

'The memory of that place makes me shudder; it is repulsive to me even now. I think I never saw such a wicked school before or since. The place was bad, wicked, filthy; and the treatment was starvation and cruelty.'

There were many such schools in Victorian Britain. Shaftesbury was happier when he went on to one of the great public schools, Harrow, and then to Oxford University.

The family mansion of the Shaftesburys is at St. Giles, Wimborne, Dorset. This great house is open to visitors. Here can be seen objects and documents connected with the life of the Earl. An interesting book for you to read is *The Young Shaftesbury*, by R. A. Sisson.

Lord Shaftesbury would be a good subject for a service in Morning Assembly. Prepare it in this order: a reading about his life and work, including his motto, 'Love – Serve'; a suitable hymn about children; a prayer you have composed yourself.

The Victorian rich called the slum dwellers and the homeless poor,
'The Great Unwashed'. How do you think people with no homes, living
in the streets, could wash themselves or their clothes? The picture
shows a night refuge for homeless women and their children. You see
the wooden coffin-like beds and the thin blankets. These would become
infested with bugs, fleas and lice. The smell of unwashed bodies
and clothes in such shelters night after night was unforgettable.

Now read this letter printed in *The Times* newspaper of 5th July
1849. It was signed by 54 poor and desperate Londoners living in a
district of Soho.

'Sur,

May we beg and beseech your proteckshion and power. We are Sur,
as it may be, living in a Wilderness, so far as the rest of London
knows anything of us, or as the rich and great people care about. We
live in muck and filthe. We aint got no privez, no dustbins, no
drains, no water splies, and no drain or suer in the whole place. The
Suer Company, in Greek Street, Soho Square, all great, rich and
powerfool men, take no notice watsomedever of our complaints. The
Stenche of a Gully-hole is disgustin. We al of us suffur, and
numbers are ill, and if the Colera comes Lord help us . . .'

What 3 public services, necessary for health in towns, were
lacking in this district? What did the people fear would happen to
them? All through the 19th century there was a demand for water and
'privez' in the overcrowded districts. Before 1856 sewers emptied into
the River Thames near the city. Yet millions of gallons of water were
drawn off daily for people's needs.

In the main streets of towns water was laid on to the houses. In some districts there was a street 'stand pipe' like the one in this picture. (You may still find these in some country villages and near beach huts or caravan sites.) But many people still drew water from the old street pumps.

Cholera was one of the diseases feared by Victorians. In 1854 many people were dying from this in a district in Soho. A Dr. John Snow went to work to find the cause. He found that no one in the local brewery was ill — all drank beer. The people in the work-house were mostly free from infection — they had their own well. The rest drew water from the pump in Broad Street. Then a lady died from cholera in Hampstead. She drank water fetched daily from the Broad Street Pump. Dr. Snow found out the cause of the trouble. The pump water was infected by sewage draining into it.

In the hot summer of 1855 the smell from the River Thames was so bad it was known as 'The Great Stink'. In the Houses of Parliament by the river members found it difficult to breathe. Curtains soaked in chloride of lime were hung over the windows to clear the air.

You would probably guess what is happening in this picture. It is 1856 and the new sewers are being built. These carried the sewage away from London for 14 miles (22·5km) before it flowed into the river.

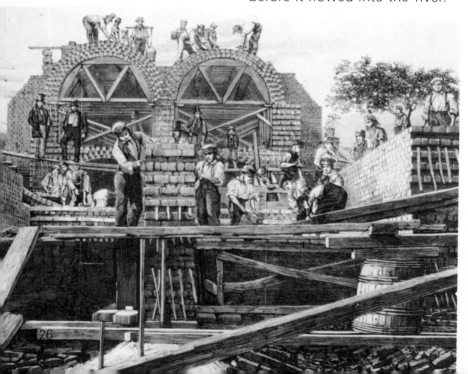

Find out:
where the water
supply to your home
comes from;
how the sewage is dealt
with; how people
are now protected from
the following diseases:
smallpox,
diphtheria,
typhus,
typhoid and
cholera.

The business world Where was this shop in Nottingham? To whom did it belong? What is lettered across the window? This was the first shop of Jesse Boot. It was a success. His method was to buy in bulk cheaply and sell to his customers at reduced prices.

Left fatherless at 10 he first helped his mother in their struggle to make a living in a little shop. They sold herbs for simple medicines. By the time he died in 1931 he was no longer plain Jesse Boot. He was Baron Trent of Nottingham. He owned a chain of shops known as Boots the Chemists. It was he who gave grants of money for what is now Nottingham University.

Jesse Boot was only one of many young men in the 19th century who made fortunes in the business world. They were men of little schooling, money or influence. But they had self-reliance, courage and a will to work hard.

Have you ever shopped at any of these great department stores: John Lewis, Peter Robinson, Derry and Toms and Swan and Edgar in London, Bainbridge's in Newcastle, Robert Sayle in Cambridge, Jenners in Edinburgh, Colmers in Bath?
These and many others had their beginnings in the 19th century.

William Edgar came to London to seek his fortune from his home on a farm at Longtown, Cumberland. It is said that he started by trading in a street market and slept under his stall at night. He made a friend of another trader, John Swan. When Edgar was only 21, and Swan 35, they boldly went into partnership and opened a shop in Piccadilly in 1812.

AMERICAN LADIES AND GENTLEMEN

Are respectfully invited to inspect the Largest, Choicest, and Cheapest Stock of SILKS, FURS, COSTUMES, and GENERAL DRAPERY GOODS at the Lowest Ready-money Prices in the Kingdom.

SWAN AND EDGAR,

By Appointment to Her Majesty the Queen,

WHOLESALE AND RETAIL WAREHOUSEMEN,

9, 10, 11, Piccadilly, & 39 to 53, Regent Street,

LONDON.

DEPARTMENTS.

SILKS.	COSTUMES.	HOSIERY.
VELVETS.	MANTLES.	HABERDASHERY.
SHAWLS.	MATERIALS.	RIBBONS.
FURS.	GLOVES.	MILLINERY.
LACE.	DRAPERY.	OUTFITTING.

Bonnets, Black Silks, at Wholesale Prices.

DRESSES MADE ON THE PREMISES AT THE SHORTEST NOTICE BY EXPERIENCED HANDS.

ESTABLISHED SIXTY YEARS.

136

From this trade card printed by Swan and Edgar in 1872, you will see how their small beginnings grew into a great department store where Queen Victoria was pleased to do some of her shopping. A handkerchief dropped in the store one day by one of the Queen's children is still in the possession of one of the great-great-great-grandchildren of Mr. Edgar.

Puzzle out from this trade card:
— whether ready-to-wear clothes were on sale at this time
— whether terms were for cash or credit
— what horse-drawn traffic is in the streets.

The name, Swan and Edgar has been in Piccadilly for more than 150 years.

Write 2 paragraphs in your Journal to describe the street scene Swan and Edgar would see from their windows a hundred years ago and the traffic and people they would see if they returned today.

1.—The Shop is opened at 6.30 A.M. Junior Assistants must be in the Shop to attend to their Duties at 6.45. Young Men sleeping on the Premises must be in the Shop, ready for the business of the day, at 7.30.

2.—Twenty minutes is allowed for Breakfast. The first party go at 8 o'clock, the second at 8.30. Everyone must be in business immediately after. Half-an-hour is allowed for Dinner. The first party go at 1 o'clock, the second at 1.40. Twenty minutes is allowed for Tea. The first party go at 5 o'clock, the second at 5.30. Twenty minutes is allowed for Supper, the time for which will vary according to the season of the year. Each Assistant will have a Partner for meals, and on no account is one to leave or be absent from the Shop before the other has returned.

3.—To avoid waste at Meals, Assistants are requested, not to accept more meat upon their plates than they require. The Waiters have orders to report unnecessary waste to the Firm. No loud talking allowed. Assistants detained from their regular parties at Meals, must have ticket signed from a Shopwalker stating time of leaving Shop.

4.—Young Men may be absent from the Shop for 10 minutes, and Young Ladies for 20 minutes, before 11 o'clock, for washing hands, &c.; after which time no Assistants allowed in their Bedrooms under any pretence whatever, without a written permission from a Shopwalker, and all lights must be extinguished twenty minutes after locking-up.

5.—Young Men are to wear Black Frock Coats and Vests, White Shirts and Black Ties. Young ladies behind Counters to wear black dresses, and the regulation white linen collar and cuffs. No unnecessary adornments are allowed.

6.—Assistants may purchase goods for themselves on Tuesdays, Thursdays, and Saturdays, before 11 A.M.; the same must be paid for at time of purchase, when 8 per cent. will be added by the Cashier to the cost price. All parcels must pass through the Entering Room, and will be delivered at night by the Commissioner on the production of the receipt.

7.—No Newspapers to be read, or Private Letters to be written during business hours. Every Assistant leaving the premises on business, must depart and return by the Trade Entrance, and state to the Doorkeeper where they are going.

8.—Assistants are required to assist each other in making sales by finding and folding up goods, and by keeping the Counters clear.

9.—All Dressing-out must be completed by 10.30 A.M. at the latest, and on Saturdays no goods to be removed until 2 o'clock, or from the windows until within ten minutes of closing time, without special permission.

10.—After a Bill has been made out to a Customer, it must be carefully examined by a Buyer or Shopwalker, or in absence of both, the first hand in the Department, who must compare prices marked with the prices charged. In case of loss through being incorrectly examined, the deficit must be equally borne between the seller and the one who signs.

11.—No deviation from the proper selling price marked on the goods is to be made without special permission. In quoting for short lengths or remnants reference must always be made to the Buyer of the Department.

12.—Cheques to be signed in the Counting House, or by the Manager, before being passed into Cash Desk.

13.—Any Assistant allowing a Customer to go away unserved without first appealing to the Buyer will be subject to instant dismissal.

14.—To prevent misunderstanding with regard to the amount of Money Customers may put down in payment of their Bills, the amount should be written down on the left-hand corner of the Bill, and called over in the presence of the Customer.

Swan and Edgar opened a hostel for their young assistants, and each was given a printed set of rules. This is a photograph of rules 1–14.

Read them carefully, then in your Journal draw up a timetable for an assistant's working day in the 1870s. Find out what hours are worked by shop assistants today (a hundred years later), and enter these opposite the first timetable. Compare the two.

It was not until 1884 that a law forbade employment of the under 18s for more than $13\frac{1}{2}$ hours daily.

Your family groceries today are bought pre-packed in packets, tins and jars. Their contents have been checked at the factories for cleanliness and quality. All this care over the marketing of your food has come about in this century. In Victorian times food was displayed in bulk, unprotected on shop counters. Customers waited while butter, cheese and lard were cut from great slabs and weighed up for them on scales on the counter. For pickles, vinegar, treacle and milk it was necessary to take jugs or jars to the grocers.

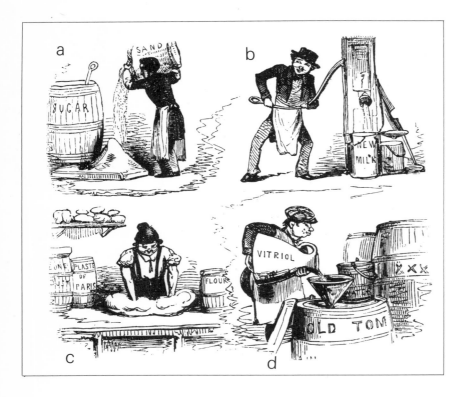

There was much cheating and fraud in the marketing of food and drink. From this cartoon of 1845 ca[n] you discover what is being mixed in with:

a sugar
b milk
c flour
d beer?

Why do you think this is being done?

Tea was measured out from big canisters filled from the foil-lined plywood chests straight from India or China. Before the sugar you know as cube or lump came into use, refined (or white) sugar was produced in the form of a 'loaf' or cone like the one photographed here. It weighed 14lb. (6·35kg). The loaf had to be broken up into pieces with sugar cutters.

One man who was disgusted with all the dirt and dishonesty in the food trade was John Sainsbury. He began work as a grocer's boy in the New Cut, Lambeth, earning 1s 6d per week. The time came when he was able to open a shop of his own. He based his business on honest trading and cleanliness.

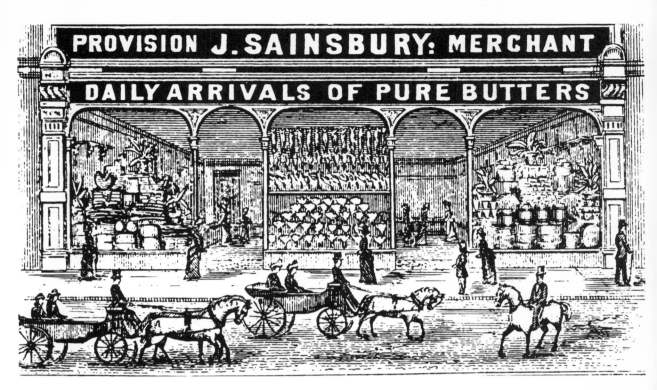

Who was the owner of this shop in High Road, Balham, in 1888? What traffic is in the road? Here is the 9th shop of John Sainsbury.

This shop was opened at the time when the first supplies of frozen meat were arriving. The meat was brought in the new refrigerator ships from the Argentine, Australia, and New Zealand. The shop was to have the new substitute for butter, called 'margarine', the recent invention of a French scientist.

The Sainsbury shops were noted for their cleanliness. There were mosaic floors laid by Italian craftsmen and tiled walls which could be washed. Working hours for shop assistants were long. Sainsbury's like other provision shops were open from 7·30 a.m. till 9·15 p.m. but on Fridays they remained open until 10·45 p.m. and on Saturdays (when most workmen were paid) until midnight. The staff worked on until 2 a.m. scrubbing floors and counters. The firm now has its own farms, bakeries and packing stations, and some 250 shops and supermarkets.

Collect and sort for your Journal, advertisements, labels and pictures of any businesses about which you have read on pages 27 to 31. Possibly in your district there may be others dating back to the reign of Victoria, firms like Marks and Spencer, Cadbury, Bovril Ltd., Colman's, Chivers, Pears and Lever Bros. In your spare time make a study of any such firm. Record it all in your Journal.

Many workers in towns were able to join the new Friendly Societies. These offered friendship and companionship. They cared for a member and his family in poverty, sickness and death. The banner of one of these Friendly Societies, the Ancient Order of Foresters, is pictured here. Find on it the initials A.O.F. Look for the motto of the Society and at the top, the all-seeing eye of God the Creator. There are other symbols or signs on the banner. These had special meanings for the members.

The A.O.F. was founded in 1834. Clubs or 'Courts' as they were called, were formed all over the country. Each court had a President called the Chief Ranger. To which Court did this banner belong? Friendly Societies still continue their work in some of our towns today. Is there one in your town or district?

The friendly societies

A London scene in the 1880s The church on the right is St-Martin-In-The-Fields which gave its name to the picture. The artist was William Logsdail and the painting is now in the Tate Gallery in London. Find:

- a brewer's dray loaded with beer barrels and drawn by two shire horses
- the curious cab, known as a Hansom, with its brass candle lamps. Where do the passengers sit? What does the driver wear as protection against the rain?
- the horse-drawn bus in the distance
- the milk cart. Just behind is a hackney coach with luggage on top.
- the gas street lamps (only a few London streets were already lit by electricity)
- the newspaper seller. He wears a bowler hat, by then very fashionable
- the little flower seller in large worn boots and ragged clothes
- a mounted policeman wearing a sword and another policeman standing nearby
- a woman street-trader selling oranges to a roadman
- a lady and her small daughter. The lady wears a full-length, fur-trimmed coat. It has the tight-fitting bodice and the bustle fashionable at that time.

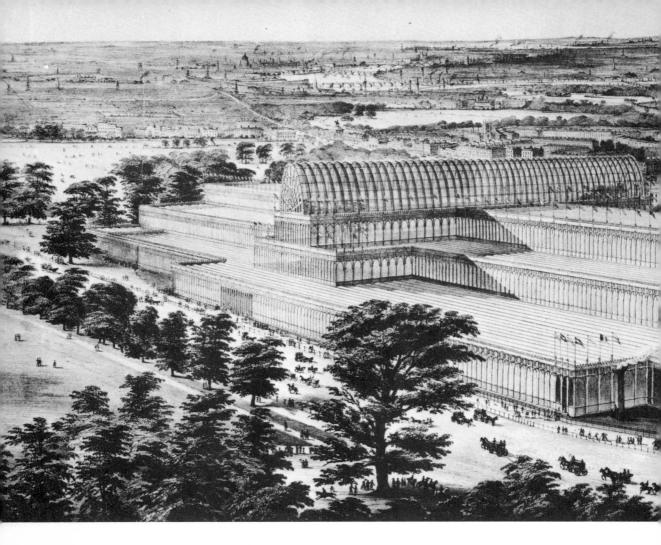

The great exhibition

You are looking now at the glass building put up in Hyde Park, London f
the Great Exhibition of 1851. This was the first International Exhibition ev
to be held. It was the idea of Prince Albert, the Queen's husband. By lookir
at the carriages in the foreground you will get some idea of its vast size. Behir
the building is mid-19th century London. You will see at this time there we
no multi-storey buildings, but search for:

— the dome of St. Paul's cathedral (top left of picture)
— the River Thames to the right of this, and arched bridges each now replace
   1 the nearest, Waterloo Bridge, built by John Rennie in 1813
   2 Blackfriars Bridge
   3 the iron bridge at Southwark, built by Rennie in 1818
— many factory chimneys and rows of houses behind the glass palace.

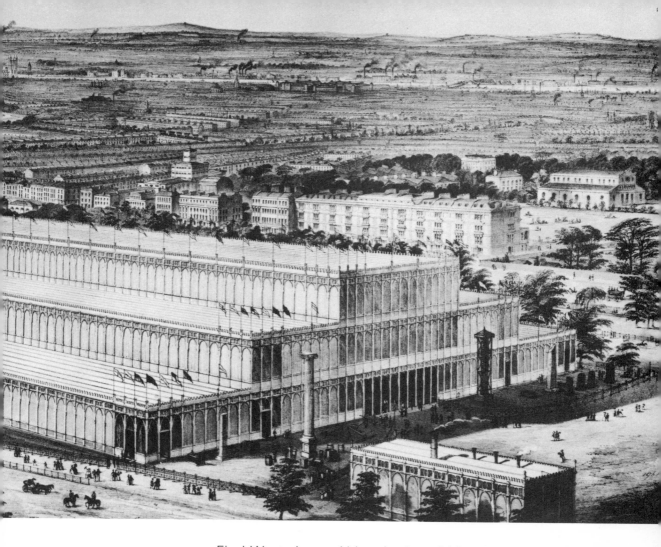

Find Westminster Abbey in the middle distance, and behind
this the fine buildings of the Houses of Parliament. These
were planned by Sir Charles Barry and Augustus Welby
Pugin, two famous Victorian architects. There had been a
terrible fire in 1834 which had burned down nearly all the
old Palace of Westminster where Parliament used to meet.
Westminster Hall escaped the fire and this medieval building
still stands.

In the British section of the Exhibition steam-driven
machines interested the crowds, for this was the great age of
steam power. Steam, from coal-fired boilers now drove
machinery in the factories, the new railway engines, some
ships at sea, and engines in farm use for threshing corn.

This is a view inside the building. The magazine *Punch* christened it
'The Crystal Palace'. Notice:
— two of the elm trees on the site, enclosed in the building
— the graceful iron gates made at Coalbrookdale, a centre of the
   iron industry. (These gates still stand in Hyde Park.)
— beyond the gates the beautiful crystal fountain of polished cut glass
— the men in uniform on duty at the gates. What are they called?
Among those who organised tours to the Great Exhibition was Thomas
Cook. He was the founder of the now world-famous travel agency.
Over 6 million people went to see this Great Exhibition.

The Crystal Palace was built in only 9 months, and a curious story lies behind its planning. 245 designs had been received from home and abroad. Then a certain Joseph Paxton decided at the very last to send in a design. Paxton, a country lad from Bedfordshire, had risen to become head gardener, friend and adviser to the Duke of Devonshire. At the Duke's home at Chatsworth, he built a glass conservatory which was large enough for the Duke's carriage to drive through. Then he built a lily house of glass and iron for a rare tropical water-lily which had leaves of 5 feet (1·5 metres) across.

Paxton's plan for the Exhibition building was for a palace of glass and metal, not brick and stone, but a place of light and pleasure. He had to take into account the effect of heat, storms, condensation and security, for the building was to house treasures from many nations. His remarkable design was accepted. What do you learn from these entries from the Queen's Journal for 1851?

18th February 'After breakfast we drove with the 5 children to look at the Crystal Palace . . . really now one of the wonders of the world. The building is so light and graceful, in spite of its immense size . . . Many of the exhibits have arrived. We were . . . cheered by 2,000 workmen . . . it made me feel proud and happy.'

29th April 'We drove to the Exhibition . . . and remained about 2 hours and $\frac{1}{2}$. I came back quite dead beat and my head really bewildered by the myriads of beautiful and wonderful things which . . . dazzled one's eyes . . . We . . . examined the French part . . . looked also at the Italian, Spanish, Portuguese and German part. The Austrian section is nearly finished . . . There are lovely embroideries from Switzerland. Russia is far behind as the ships were frozen in and could not bring the things sooner.'

1st May
the day of the opening
of the Exhibition) 'This day is one of the greatest and most glorious days of our lives, with which to my joy the name of my beloved Albert is for ever associated.'

In the Victoria and Albert Museum is this season ticket to the Exhibition.
What is its number?
To whom did it belong?

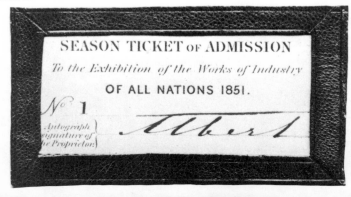

SEASON TICKET of ADMISSION
To the Exhibition of the Works of Industry
OF ALL NATIONS 1851.
Nᵒ 1
Autograph
signature of
the Proprietor:

Ten years after the Great Exhibition Prince Albert died suddenly from typhoid fever. He was a prince of Saxe-Coburg in Germany and a man of great ability. The Queen had relied greatly on his help and advice.

High on his memorial in Hyde Park is this 14 feet (4·27 metres) bronze statue. Prince Albert was a member of the Most Noble Order of the Garter. You will see he is wearing the Collar of the Order and the Garter itself below the left knee. He holds in his right hand the catalogue of the Great Exhibition. This Exhibition had been his vision and much of its success was due to him.

Prince Albert is looking across the Kensington Road to the Albert Hall and the great centres of learning beyond. Here are museums, colleges and schools built on a site bought for the purpose with the large profits from the Great Exhibition. One day you may be a student at one of the colleges there: The Imperial College of Science and Technology, The Royal College of Art, or The Royal College of Music. Perhaps you may visit one of the famous museums of Science, Geology or Natural History, the Victoria and Albert, shown in the picture.

Now plan an advertisement to attract visitors to the Great Exhibition of 1851.

The post

Six years after the Great Exhibition, pillar boxes like the one below first appeared in the streets. This street pillar box was only 4 feet (1·22 metres) high and 21 inches (0·538 metres) wide. Find:

— the Royal cipher, V.R.
— the horizontal flap on one side of the domed top. This covered the posting slot.
— the place for the 'Hours of Collection' plate
— the locking device
— the mouldings of roses, thistles, ribbons and animals' heads. This is a fine example of the Victorian love of decoration on every surface.

The demand for street pillar boxes arose after the new postage was introduced. There had been a postal service in Britain for over 200 years, but it had been the custom for the person who received the letter to pay for it. The cost had been based on distance and the number of sheets of paper sent. Many people were too poor to pay for letters sent to them. For example a letter sent from Preston to Lancaster (about 20 miles or 32 km) could cost 2s.

In 1840 Parliament adopted the plan of Sir Rowland Hill: a letter sheet which was folded, sealed and could be sent anywhere in Britain for a penny. This was good news for people working away from their families. If they could read and write they could now afford to send news home. Then Rowland Hill had the idea of the first stamp:

'a bit of paper . . . covered with a glutinous (gummed) wash, which the user might, by applying a little moisture, attach to the back of the letter'.

A travelling Post Office on the London to Birmingham Railway 1838

So came the first gummed postage sta[mp]
in the world, the famous Penny Black
On the black background is the head [of]
the young Queen Victoria. Which way [is]
she facing? On present day stamps, wh[ich]
way does the Sovereign face? Look i[n your]
stamp album to see which way other
sovereigns face. Is this the same as on
our coins?

Notice there is no name of the
country on the Penny Black or on any [of]
our modern stamps. Our sovereign's he[ad]
on a stamp will carry our letters anywhere in the world. The check letters [S]
and C found in the bottom corners of
this Penny Black show where the stam[p]
was cut from the sheet of 240 stamps
(20 rows of 12 stamps) for there was [no]
perforation till 1854. The left-hand
letter S shows this stamp was row 19
(A to S) and the right-hand letter C
shows it was the 3rd stamp in the row[.]
These letters were stamped on by hand
and collectors look for special differen[ces]
which add to the value of the stamp.

There now came a demand for
gummed envelopes. These 2 children
are operating an envelope machine
which could gum and fold 60
envelopes a minute.

Measure up a pillar box bearing the
Royal Cipher E II R and draw it to scal[e]
in your Journal, side by side with a
scale drawing of the Victorian pillar
box on page 39. With a friend start
a pillar box treasure hunt, to find how
many different ones are in service.
Draw each in your Journal and note
where you found it.

The police

Read this notice and find out what had been happening in Stansted in 1877. You will see that then as now, the police had trouble with vandals. How were they described on the notice?

There was no police force in the British Isles until 1814. Then Sir Robert Peel, the Secretary

Stansted Gas Company.
£1 REWARD.

Whereas some evil disposed boys are constantly Throwing Stones and

BREAKING THE GLASS IN THE STREET LAMPS.

The above Reward will be given to any one giving information that will lead to the Conviction of the offendors.

JAMES MARSH, Secretary.

STANSTED, OCTOBER 27th, 1877.

H. COLLINGS AND CO.'S STEAM PRINTING WORKS, BISHOP STORTFORD.

for Ireland, tried out a police force in that country. It was called the Irish Constabulary. Fifteen years later he founded the Metropolitan Police Force. At first policemen were very unpopular. They were nicknamed 'Peelers' or 'Bobbies'. Can you guess why? They had a tough time against villains in the dimly-lit London streets. Many were killed in riots or by thugs.

In the year 1839 town and county police forces were formed. Look at this photograph of Ipswich Police Constables in 1863, in their uniforms which were dark blue. Shortly afterwards their top hats were replaced by helmets. You will see that all the policemen have neatly-trimmed beards and side-whiskers, and carry truncheons. Find the two who wear medals. Perhaps they had been in the army and fought in the Crimean War, or the Indian Mutiny.

Punishments were harsh even for children. Read what they could expect for playing with tops in the street.

'The pegtop season having apparently set in with its usual severity constables are to capture and bring to the police station all the tops they can lay their hands upon and also, as opportunity offers, to explain to the children the penalty (14 days imprisonment) they are liable to for thus acting.'

Now in the next police notice read of another problem in the streets in 1891. The bicycle was a recent invention and the streets were still filled with horse-drawn traffic.

'The attention of the Force is called to the rapid pace at which bicycles are propelled through the streets. They are to do everything in their power to discourage this dangerous practice. . .'

Both these notices come from the General Orders of Ipswich Borough Police.

Do you like detective stories? These began to be popular after the first Detective Force was raised in London in 1842. The most famous 19th century writer of such stories was Sir Arthur Conan Doyle. You will have heard of Sherlock Holmes his great detective hero. He is still so popular that Sherlock Holmes' Societies are now run in many countries in the world.

In this photograph you can see a room which has been set up to his memory in the Sherlock Holmes pub in Northumberland Avenue, London. It is a model of the room in which he worked, exactly as described in the books about him.

Someone in your school may have a parent who is a police officer or a detective. Ask him to tell you about the history of the Police Force in your district.

In prison

To keep alive, many of the needy had to steal. Until 1861 stealing was one of 200 crimes for which Judges had to give the death sentence. Those condemned to death were strung up on gallows. In London this took place outside Newgate Gaol where crowds gathered to watch the hangings. Newgate has gone and the Old Bailey (the Central Criminal Court) stands on this site, but the road outside still widens where once the crowds stood, until public hangings ceased in 1868.

In the picture you see the exercise yard at Tothill Fields Prison in London. 300 boys under 17 were imprisoned here. Can you see that some of the cell windows have shields to shut out the light? These were punishment cells. What crimes had these boys committed? Some no doubt had longed for adventure like young Edward Jones.

Edward, living with his parents in a room up a staircase in Bell Yard, had one interest, Buckingham Palace. He found a way to get in. He had a wonderful time. He slept in one of the fine beds. He sat on the throne. He was once found under the Queen's sofa. They could not keep him out. So to teach him a lesson he was sent to prison.

Look at this schoolroom in Tothill Fields Prison. Notice:
— the long desks and forms
— the quill pens
— the row of inkwells.
During their time in prison these boys had the chance to learn to read and write.

What happen to boys and girls who break the law today?

Do you recognise the prison below? Why do you think babies and toddlers are here? What do you notice about the clothes the mothers and children are wearing? These mothers are prisoners also serving sentences at Tothill Fields Prison in Victorian times.

This view inside Holloway Prison shows:
— prisoners seated in curious box-like seats picking oakum
— behind them in numbered compartments prisoners are working
  the treadmill.

Oakum was used for caulking the seams between planks on the decks of
ships and for stopping leaks. Prisoners had to pick to pieces old
tarred ropes from sailing ships. This was called 'picking oakum'.
You will see the heaps near the prisoners' feet. It was rough work.
It rubbed their finger-tips raw and split their nails.

The treadmill was a number of revolving steps $7\frac{1}{2}$ inches (19 cm)
wide. Walking the treadmill you remained in one place, but because of
the revolving steps you were forced to climb on the spot. The time was
for 2 periods of 3 hours a day, with 15 minutes on and 5 minutes off.

When Holloway was built in 1849, these words were inscribed on
the foundation stone:

'May God preserve the city of London
and make this place a terror to evil-doers.'

Holloway, like Wandsworth, Brixton and Pentonville and other prisons
built in the middle years of the 19th century, is still in use.

Up to 1891 even poor parents had to pay a few pence each week towards their children's education. It was usually 2d a week for one child, 3d for two and 1d each for the others in the family. Some of the poorer families found it very difficult to find the school pence each week. From the school log-books we can find frequent entries about this:

'25 March 1887 James Noble sent home for school pence.'

'9 Sept. 1884 20 children sent home this afternoon for school money.'

'4 Nov. 1887 3 Farrow children sent home for school pence this week owing several weeks' back money.'

At what age can you leave school? At the end of the 19th century the school-leaving age was raised to 12. What do you think the school-leaving age might be at the end of this century?

The photograph above shows children at one of our state schools which started in 1870. Each of these was called a 'Board School' because it was controlled by a Board of Managers. You may still find, if you search, the words 'Board School' lettered on the walls of old school buildings. Before State schools began, some societies started schools. The National Society gave its name to one group, called 'National Schools'. You read of another on page 23.

In Scotland plans had been made as early as 1696 for a school and a school-master for every parish. So Scotland was ahead of England and Wales.

The Salvation Army

Down the Ratcliffe Highway, Stepney, in 1882 marches one of the
first Salvation Army Bands. You can see:
— bandsmen in uniforms which were blue and red as they are today
— the Salvation Army flag. Its motto is 'Blood and Fire'.
— the Salvation Army lassie, right at the back, with bonnet and
   tambourine
— behind the houses the tall masts of ships in the London Docks
— the public house (called 'The Sailors' Rest'), and the pawnbroker's
   shop with the sign of 3 brass balls. The locals called them
   'swinging dumplings'.
The pawning of goods to buy liquor was one of the evils the
Salvation Army fought.

The founder of the Salvation Army, William Booth, was apprenticed for 6 years in 1842 to a pawnbroker in Nottingham. Poor people came to the shop with all kinds of goods on which the pawnbroker lent them money. The pawnbroker issued tickets for the goods stating the length of time he would keep them. If the owner did not buy them back in that time, the pawnbroker was allowed to sell the goods at a profit. In some towns you may still see the sign of 3 brass balls over a pawnbroker's shop.

William Booth made friends with the young 'toughs' of the district where he worked. He persuaded them one Sunday to go with him to a church,

'All unwashed, uncombed, their clothes ragged and their
shoes broken, a tribe of them marched down the aisle
to the front seats.'

This upset some members of the congregation, so Booth and his friends were asked to sit in future where they could not be seen. Booth thought about this. If these sort of people were not welcome at a church service then Booth would take a service to them. So was born the idea of the Salvation Army.

In time the work of the Salvation Army spread to fight the evils caused by drunkenness and gambling. It gave help to the hungry, the homeless and the desperate — 'Soup, Soap and Salvation' the people christened it. When Booth died at the age of 83 the Salvation Army was working in almost every country in the world.

You may have listened to one of the Salvation Army music groups, The Joy Strings, on the radio or seen the group on Television. If you live in a town find out where the Salvation Army Head-quarters are. Perhaps it could be arranged for one of their leaders to come and talk to your class about the work of the Salvation Army in the world today.

In your Journal head a page, General Booth and the Salvation Army. Then write down what you have learnt from pages 47 and 48. Leave room to add anything else you can find out. Illustrate your work with drawings.

Famine and emigration

At the end of the 1840s the town of Liverpool more than doubled its population.

It was not possible to house and feed the thousands of starving people who poured into the city. Slum dwellings and old disused cellars were soon crowded. In some cases up to 40 people tried to find shelter in one cellar.

To stop the spread of disease, Dr. William Duncan, the first Medical Officer of Health, had the cellars cleared and filled with sand. From where did all these people come? The story starts in Ireland.

In Ireland there were many small farms. On these very few labourers were employed. Three-quarters of the Irish labourers did no regular job at all. They had no money to buy food produced on Irish farms so they lived on the potatoes they grew themselves. The farmers, to pay their rents, had to sell their produce abroad. Many of their land-lords lived away from Ireland and were called 'absentee landlords'.

You will still find in Ireland small homesteads like this one in Co. Galway. Sometimes ruins of earlier cabins stand nearby. It was often easier to build a new cabin rather than repair the old. Many of the poorer cabins had only a single window-less room. Fires were kept burning from dried turf cut out from the peat bogs.

In the year 1845 a strange new disease attacked the Irish potato crop. Within a few days of digging up, the potatoes rotted. There was soon famine in the land. You have probably helped to raise money for the starving in some parts of the world. In the 1840s it would have been the victims of the Irish potato famine who needed your help.

Soup kitchens like the one below were set up to provide soup for the hungry and penniless. These poor wretched people crowded into the cities and tried to enter the workhouses, which were forced to close their doors against so many.

The English Government had not understood what was going on in Ireland. When the potato crop failed the Government sent over supplies of Indian corn (maize) from the United States. But this was not enough. Thousands died of starvation.

John Mitchell, who was arrested in 1848 for taking part in a rebellion in Ireland, and sentenced to be transported, wrote a Jail Journal. Read in these lines from the introduction how, in the famine years:

    'Families, when all was eaten and no hope left, took their last look
    at the sun, built up their cottage doors that none might see them
    die nor hear their groans, and were found weeks afterwards,
    skeletons on their own hearths.'

From Mitchell's Jail Journal we also learn that 'starving wretches were transported as convicts for stealing vegetables.' For even while people were dying of starvation, food which they could not afford to buy was being exported from Irish farms. England received from Ireland farm produce worth 15 million pounds in each of the famine years.

Thousands of wretched penniless ragged and diseased Irish refugees
fled to towns in England, Scotland and Wales. Many travelled crammed
into empty coal ships returning to Cardiff from Cork.

In the 5 years following the potato famine thousands of Irish
emigrated to the United States, Canada, Australia and New Zealand.
Some old unseaworthy ships were brought from their moorings to carry
the poorer emigrants cheaply across the seas. We read of emigrants on
these ships screaming for hours through fear in a storm, of the misery
of seasickness in the crowded holds, of the raw uneatable food, of
cholera and typhus outbreaks. Thousands died and were buried at sea.

Study this picture of an emigration ship leaving Liverpool in 1850.
Notice:
— the women's shawls
— the many emigrants who are barefoot
— their few possessions.

Do you think these emigrants are well equipped for a new life in
a strange land? This was a great period of emigration from all
parts of the British Isles.

In your Journal draw or paint 6 pictures to illustrate the story of
the Irish Potato Famine. Give a title to each picture.

The stories of the unseaworthy ships at sea and the dreadful loss of life worried at least one man — Samuel Plimsoll. It was true that fine ships like the tea-clipper *Cutty Sark* (still to be seen at Greenwich) were being built. But Plimsoll collected tragic stories from sailors at the docks. They told of shipyards which patched and plugged and bolted ships which should long have been broken up: of ships with rotten hulks and rotten beams. There were ships that had been cut in two and lengthened beyond their strength in order to carry extra cargo. There were ships that went to sea overloaded in winter gales. The owners of such ships saw that they were well insured. So they actually made a profit if the ships were lost.

Samuel Plimsoll, as a member of Parliament, struggled for years to right these wrongs. It was not however until 1890 that the Government ordered a loadline to be shown on the hull of every ocean-going ship. This loadline was, and still is, known as the Plimsoll Line. It is part of the device shown here called the Plimsoll Mark. On each side of the Plimsoll Line are letters showing which authority issued the mark to that particular ship, e.g. L.R. for Lloyd's Register.

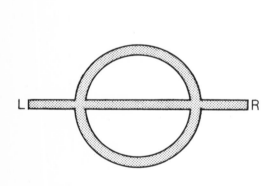

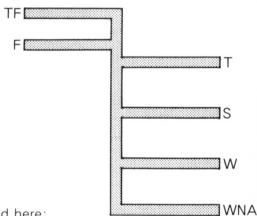

As you see the level of the loadline varies as explained here:

TF — Tropical Freshwater
F — Freshwater elsewhere
T — Tropical seas
S — Summer in all except tropical seas
W — Winter in other seas
WNA — Winter North Atlantic

When you visit docks look for the Plimsoll Mark which you will find amidships. Copy the device and its explanation into your Journal and add notes on Samuel Plimsoll and his work.

Doctors and nurses

Have you any idea what this apparatus could be?
Because of its invention many people lived
who might have died in agony.
Now read of its use on a
Royal occasion.

In August 1871 Queen Victoria was
at Balmoral Castle in Scotland. There she
became ill with an abcess under her right arm.
Her doctor sent to Edinburgh for the famous
surgeon Joseph Lister. He decided that he
would have to lance the abcess.

The Queen wrote in her Journal:
'I feel dreadfully nervous
as I feel pain so badly.'

Lister however was careful to freeze the
abcess with ether to prevent the Queen
feeling pain. During the operation, a new
invention of Lister's was used. This was the
germ-killing carbolic spray you see in the photograph.
The idea of germs causing infection was new at this time.

Some 20 years before this, James Simpson, was
experimenting with chloroform. He used it as an
anaesthetic in operations. In our modern world
anaesthetics are taken for granted, but a little over
a 100 years ago operations took place with no
anaesthetics. The patient was strapped down fully
conscious to a table. Many patients just died from
shock or from infected wounds.

Here are 2 facts for you to remember:
Simpson made surgery painless.
Lister made surgery safe.

Try to borrow from your library the interesting book,
Joseph Lister by F. Cartwright, and read more about
the work of this great surgeon.

Make a sketch of the carbolic spray for your
Journal. Add notes about Joseph Lister and
James Simpson.

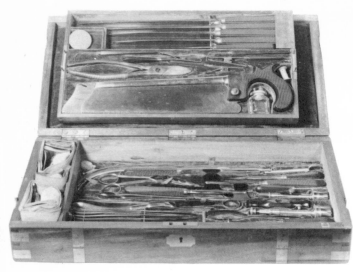

How many of these instruments can you name? What type of person might have used them? This case, like the carbolic spray, is in the Wellcome Medical Museum, London. It belonged to Dr. Usher Evans. These very instruments were used by him on the battlefields of the Crimea. There in 1854 the British were fighting the Russians.

Find the Crimea on a map. Then find and read *'The Charge of the Light Brigade,'* a poem written by Tennyson. The charge took place at the Battle of Balaclava, in the Crimea.

This gold and diamond brooch also travelled out to the Crimea. You can gather something of its history by looking at the inscription, the royal crown and cipher V.R., the word on the scroll, and by reading this letter.

'Windsor Castle Jan 1856

    Dear Miss Nightingale,

I need hardly repeat to you how warm my admiration is for your services, which are fully equal to those of my dear and brave soldiers. I am, however, anxious of marking my feelings in a manner which I trust will be agreeable to you and therefore send you with this letter a brooch. . .

             VICTORIA R.'

To whom was it sent?
By whom was it sent?
From where was it sent?
Why was it sent?

    Behind this brooch and the pictures on the next two pages lies an astonishing story.

Miss Nightingale was a national heroine. Pictures and statues were made of her. Her likeness was even carved as this ship's figurehead. This can still be seen in the *Cutty Sark* at Greenwich. Florence Nightingale's parents were very wealthy. She was intelligent and well-educated. The gay life of her friends bored her for she wanted to be a nurse. She wanted to improve the conditions of squalor and misery of most hospitals at that time. There was no proper training for nurses so to gain experience Miss Nightingale travelled abroad. Her parents were terrified, for girls of her class did not work in hospitals then.

Now read part of a letter which Miss Nightingale received on 15th October 1854.

'Dear Miss Nightingale,

You will have seen in the papers that there is a great deficiency (shortage) of nurses at Scutari. . . none but male nurses having ever been admitted to military hospitals. I receive numbers of offers from ladies to go out, but they have no conception (idea) of what a hospital is, nor of the nature of its duties. . . Would you listen to the request to go and superintend the whole thing? You would of course have authority over all the nurses. . . I know you will come to a wise decision. . .

        ever yours,

        Sidney Herbert (Secretary-At-War)'

This was a challenge that Florence was glad to accept. She would have read in *The Times* newspaper the week before, a despatch from their war reporter, William Russell. He wrote about the big military hospital at Scutari in Turkey which had been prepared for the wounded.

'It is possible to provide for the reception of about 6,000 sick or wounded. It was a moving sight yesterday to see the wounded borne to the hospital. From dawn to evening the labour was incessant, and the officers and medical men seemed perfectly worn out with fatigue. The soldiers attend upon each other and directly a man is able to walk, he is made useful in nursing . . . Everywhere there are noise and discomfort, with a mixture of dirt and unclean smells which are unavoidable in such places.'

When Florence Nightingale arrived at Scutari with 40 helpers on November 5th 1854, a third great battle, Inkerman, was being fought up in the Crimea. She found the hospital was short of food, water, beds, blankets, clothing, fuel, splints, bandages, drugs, sanitary arrangements, doctors and anaesthetics, and there were fleas, lice and rats.

The Times newspapers of October 9, November 13 and November 23 published the long lists of dead and wounded from the battles of Alma, Balaclava and Inkerman. Perhaps the name of one of your ancestors appeared among them.

At first Miss Nightingale had a fierce struggle with the army doctors who did not agree with having women in army hospitals. But in the hard winter that followed the sick and wounded poured into the hospital at Scutari. Miss Nightingale and her helpers were then badly needed. Canvas cases were stuffed with straw and placed on the floor a foot (30 cm) apart. Men lay on these in their army coats in blood, pain and filth for days before they could be given attention.

This strange vehicle, an army baggage cart was used by Miss Nightingale when she visited field hospitals in the Crimea. After the war it was brought back to England. It now rests in the Army Transport Museum at Borden, Hampshire.

When Florence Nightingale came back to England she found she was famous. A large sum of money had been collected for her. This was used to start a Training School for Nurses at St. Thomas's Hospital, London. Here was the beginning of the fine nursing profession we have today.

'Young ladies all, of every clime,
Especially of Britain,
Who wholly occupy your time
In novels or in knitting,
Whose highest skill is but to play
Sing, dance, or French to clack well,
Reflect on the example, pray,
Of excellent Miss Blackwell!'

So wrote the magazine *Punch* when Miss
Elizabeth Blackwell became news in 1849.
And who was Miss Blackwell? She lived in
the U.S.A. and was the first woman in the
world to become a doctor. In England in the
little seaside town of Aldeburgh lived
another Elizabeth whose portrait you see
here. She was bored by the life led by the
daughters of the wealthy (as Florence
Nightingale had been). So she decided she would follow the
career chosen by Miss Blackwell and become a doctor. At
first her mother wept and her father stormed. But Mr.
Garrett was finally coaxed into helping his daughter.

How to begin? At this time no woman in England could even
get a University degree. (Degrees were not given to women
at Cambridge until 1922.) The medical profession would not
allow women to train as doctors, so Elizabeth started as a
nurse. She listened to the lectures given to the medical
students.

It was 10 long years of work and struggle before
Elizabeth gained her M.D. in Paris in 1869. She was the
first woman to do so. Do you know the meaning of the letters
M.D.? Find out from a London Telephone Directory (in a
Public Library or General Post Office) where in London is
the hospital she founded and which bears her married name:
Elizabeth Garrett Anderson.

Here are books of interest which you may be able to
borrow from your library. *Florence Nightingale*, by
F. Caudill; *Lady-in-Chief*, by C. Woodham-Smith and
They Dared To Be Doctors, by M. St. Fancourt.

Explorer and missionary

If you live in Scotland or have spent holidays there you may have visited Blantyre, near Glasgow. There you will have seen the Scottish National Memorial to David Livingstone. Here in single-roomed homes 24 families once lived. They were not slum dwellings but had been planned by the local mill-owner as homes for his workers. The picture shows a corner of the room, 10 feet (3·05 metres) by 14 feet (4·30 metres), which was David's home. Here he grew up with his parents, 2 sisters and 2 brothers. You can see:

— a stove with iron kettles and a hanging cooking pot
— the bellows by the fire-place
— two chairs, pictures and a fine clock on the wall
— two candlesticks and a tea caddy
— the parents' bed in a recess on the right. Extra beds for the children
  were made up in the room at night.

Oatmeal for porridge and oatcakes was stored in a barrel. Water was drawn from a well and there was a communal washing house.

David went to the Works' school until he was 10, when he began at the cotton mill. He worked from 6 a.m. to 8 p.m. daily. After the day's work he began night school, for his ambition was to be a medical missionary. He went to Glasgow to study medicine and the Bible. In 1840 the London Missionary Society sent him to Africa. A map of that continent then had the word UNKNOWN printed across the interior, for no white man had yet explored and mapped it.

a missionary journey of 4,300 miles (6,880 km) mainly on foot, David Livingstone was the first European to cross Africa from West to East. This fine statue of him, with a Bible in his hand, stands by the Victoria Falls which he discovered and named after the Queen.

Livingstone explored the Zambesi River, met hostile tribes and lived with cannibals. He was mauled by a lion and worked to stop the Arab traders who raided villages and sold their captives as slaves. Finally after months passed with no news of him, it was reported that Livingstone had been killed. Then an adventurous reporter, H. M. Stanley (who as a boy had run away to sea from a workhouse in Denbigh, Wales) was sent by an American newspaper to find him.

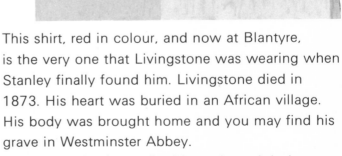

This shirt, red in colour, and now at Blantyre, is the very one that Livingstone was wearing when Stanley finally found him. Livingstone died in 1873. His heart was buried in an African village. His body was brought home and you may find his grave in Westminster Abbey.

In your Journal write the farewell address that might have been given at his funeral, telling of his life and work.

Trace or draw his statue in your Journal. An exciting book to read about Livingstone is *Trail Maker*, by R. O. Latham.

Time for enjoyment

Do you know these words from the 4th Commandment?

'Remember the sabbath day to keep it holy
six days shalt thou labour and do all thy work.'

This is what most Victorians believed to be right. But with no annual holidays the workers had little time for enjoyment. Some employers even grudged giving their workers time off on Christmas Day. Read this passage from the book, *A Christmas Carol*, by Charles Dickens. Scrooge is talking to his clerk, Bob Cratchit, on Christmas Eve 1843.

'You'll want all day tomorrow I suppose?' said Scrooge.

'If quite convenient, Sir.'

'It's not convenient,' said Scrooge, 'and it's not fair. If I was to stop half-a-crown ($12\frac{1}{2}$p) for it, you'd think yourself ill-used, I'll be bound? and yet you don't think me ill-used, when I pay a day's wages for no work.'

The clerk observed that it was only once a year. 'A poor excuse for picking a man's pocket every twenty-fifth of December!' said Scrooge . . . 'But I suppose you must have the whole day. Be here all the earlier the next morning.'

What holiday did Bob Cratchit have out of the whole year? Was it a

paid holiday? What was his wage for a six-day week? Those who cared, concerned that the workers had so little free time, worked to make changes. Saturday half-holidays were granted in 1863 and that year the Football Association was formed. In 1871 Parliament fixed Easter Monday, Whit-Monday, the first Monday in August and Boxing Day as Bank or Public Holidays. Paid annual holidays were still unthought of.

There was some time now for the workers to enjoy themselves. Many walked miles to see this cricketer play. In his sporting career, W. G. Grace scored 126 centuries and took 7,000 wickets. (Has this record been broken?) Excursion trains ran to the seaside, and to London. The Zoo, built in Regents Park, and the grand new British Museum were great attractions.

The annual fairs attracted many people. Look at this gay roundabout with its blaring organ and painted horses. It was worked by steam power.

Many women found it exciting to ride the new

safety bicycles. This advertisement of 1895 shows one of these. How does the brake work? How do you know the tyres are pneumatic? These were invented by John Dunlop in 1889. Before this, tyres were made of solid rubber. Notice that the ladies' dresses show a new fashion, leg-of-mutton sleeves.

Have you watched the Wimbledon Tennis championships on television? They began in 1877, 3 years after a Major Wingfield started the game of Lawn Tennis in England. This gave young women a chance to take part in a vigorous out-door sport, in spite of their ankle-length skirts.

61

Progress

You will have read in this book of the beginnings of much that is part of our modern life. The story of railways and steamships is told in another book, *The Transport Revolution* in the *Focus on History* series. Everything on this page too, in picture or print, had its beginnings in Victorian times.

Choose from this page, 2 subjects in which you are specially interested. Using encyclopaedias and other reference books make a detailed study of each, with illustrations, in your Journal.

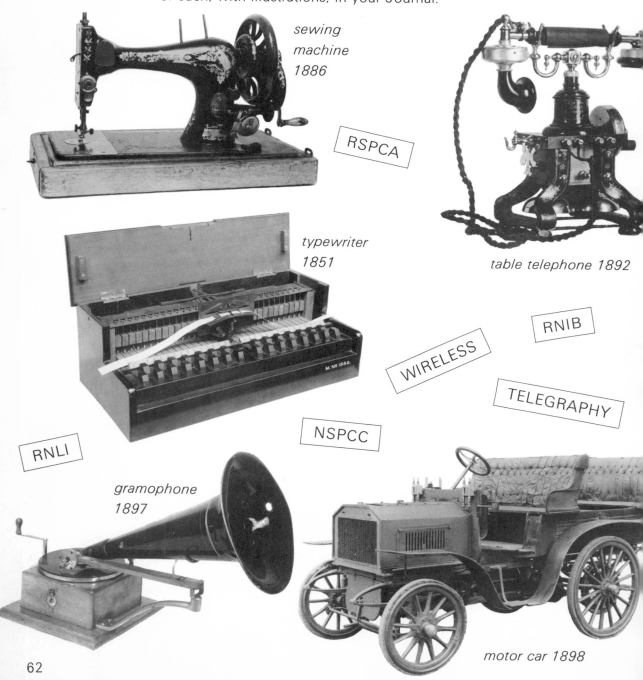

sewing machine 1886

RSPCA

table telephone 1892

typewriter 1851

RNIB

WIRELESS

TELEGRAPHY

RNLI

NSPCC

gramophone 1897

motor car 1898

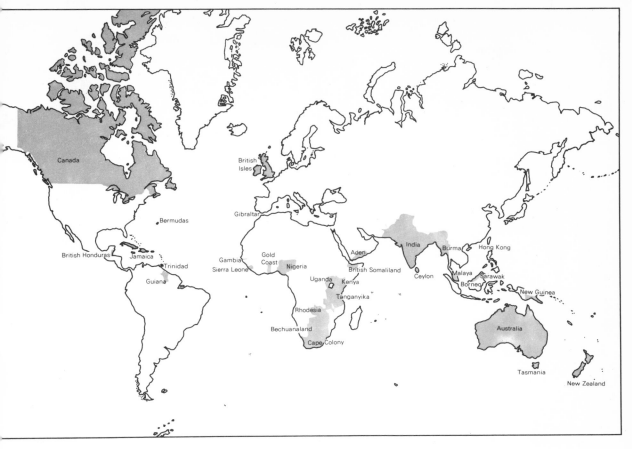

The British Empire 1901

Queen Victoria lived through into the 20th century for she died in January 1901. This book has told you a little about emigration, transportation and discovery during her lifetime. On the map above the lands which were part of the British Empire at the time of her death are shaded and named. Study the map and make a tracing of it for your Journal.

Now find a long strip of paper to make a wall frieze. On this paste as many illustrations as possible of the subjects you have read about in this book. Either draw or cut out illustrations from magazines, newspapers, catalogues, advertisements, guide books. Add cigarette cards, old picture post cards and photographs. Arrange them as you wish on the paper with a picture of Queen Victoria in the centre. Head your frieze: VICTORIAN TIMES

Index